11:11

a
poetry
collection

Written & Illustrated by
Mikaela Bauguess

First Edition: 11 November 2024

Cover illustrations and designs copyright © 2024 by Mikaela Bauguess
Interior illustrations and designs copyright © 2024 by Mikaela Bauguess

ISBN: 979-8-9918719-0-7 [paperback]
ISBN: 979-8-9918719-1-4 [hardcover]
Library of Congress Control Number: 2024922819

Published by Poetic Echo Press
Contact e-mail: mikaelawrites@outlook.com

11:11

This book is dedicated to

Mom & Dad

For always supporting my wildest ideas
and encouraging my constant creativity,
for always being on my unstable side
and never hesitating to believe in me.

Table of Contents

California Playlist

Sleep On The Floor - The Lumineers
4/20/17, page 37

You're Gonna Go Far - Noah Kahan
Carolina, page 41

When The Stars Come Out - Chris Stapleton
Wild Horse, page 65 & Salvation, page 313

Sedona - Houndmouth
Grand Canyon, page 71

Cruisin' - Huey Lewis & Gwyneth Paltrow
California, page 77

Santeria - Sublime
Another Song, page 105

May I Have This Dance - Francis and the Lights (Remix) featuring Chance the Rapper
August, page 137

Sweet Baby James - James Taylor
Let's Get Lost, page 141

The Girl - City and Colour
The Girl, page 147

Black Flies - Ben Howard
Ship, page 211

Sweet Creature - Harry Styles
Home To You, page 245

My Thoughts on You - The Band CAMINO
Thoughts, page 261

Dearly Departed - Shakey Graves featuring Esme Patterson
Hums, page 269

Rhiannon - Fleetwood Mac
Bar Singer, page 281

Introduction

This story begins in my early twenties. I was a credulous late bloomer who didn't understand that the love I watched my parents share was unusual and improbable. Love isn't always uplifting or reciprocated. Sometimes it's manipulative, lonely, and more agonizing than any physical wound ever could be. The first chapter is for the boys I pretended to love before this, the ones who took advantage of my innocent limerence, those who created my fresh fear and humble hesitance. Those were the experiences that also made me to want to leave.

I was almost twenty-three when I realized how stuck I felt in my monotonous hometown. I embodied the classic tale of a girl who felt out of place, a girl who still wanted to do empirical things. I craved more from the moment I stepped off my high school's stage with a now dusty piece of paper. A million things made it feel unattainable, but then one day, it finally happened. I got everything I had been wishing for. I got out.

My best friend and I left home and drove from North Carolina to California for no reason other than an opportunity to go. We were chasing invisible dreams without any real plans. We took a cross-country chance sharing laughs and hotel beds, holding on tight to each other's hands. We packed everything we could fit into my busted up Mustang, all of our hopes and most cherished things. Days worth of road trip playlists and conversations about the stars. I had my favorite records and he had his guitar.

He wanted to make music and I wanted to write. We both wanted to make art and run away from prosaic past lives. On the first west coast night we accidentally got too high and we danced on our new apartment balcony as we kissed under a neon sky. Out of nothing, something happened that I still can't explain. In one fleeting moment, it was quiet and everything changed.

For six months I would put up a fight for a type of love I had never felt before. I would also learn the hard way to be careful what I wished for.

Summer turned into fall as I fell mindlessly into feigned love and madness. I was stuck in a spiral of confusion, lust, force, and the undeniable ache of passion. Cheap whiskey and cigarettes became my medicine because they were his. They helped us hold on but they also helped us forget. From June until December, we lost ourselves and only pretended. When it hit us that the sunshine state couldn't fix us, we ran again. But this time instead of running to each other, we ran back home. Back to where the pain began, back into the unknown.

After 184 days of our spontaneous relocation, we started the familiar 3-day journey, but he drove so fast that we got home in only two. The 2,000 miles back were different than the 2,000 there, before we had everything and each other to lose. Silence in double hotel rooms, both beds and worlds apart. This time he didn't touch me or his guitar. We had both woken up from drunken dreams he never remembered and I had never felt a colder winter. I quietly cried as we crossed the Carolina state line. He didn't notice, but if he had, I would have lied about why. It was over even if it hadn't been said. After he dropped me off, we never spoke again.

It took me years to reread the ink and paint-stained journal pages from California and the words that remained in the wake of the worst goodbye. I ripped some of those poems out, lost for eternity to my hurt anger or the jealous boyfriends I never wrote about. I felt like my past was never valid and it seemed like requited love was just a luck of the draw. I let a false fantasy convince me to believe in a forever that never existed at all.

There were quick flickers of perfection in between the trepidation and poisonous warmth that didn't last. All I wanted was his time of day but he never wanted mine back. Much like angel numbers and wishing hours, the worst memories became tangible signs swirling all around me, even in the dark when I couldn't see. I found that I had to heal from the pain that inspired my words, and that someday, those words would become my moral guide in love. I found that falling and getting back up are inevitable and which of them to do will always be my choice. But most importantly, I found my lost and stifled voice.

It's been seven years now of learning life's hardest lessons, but even now, I still make wishes at 11:11.

11:11

a
poetry
collection

~~based
on a
true story~~

I. The Muse

Lesson For Later

When I was little my parents told me that anything could be mine if I wished for it hard enough. I would look into the sky, crossing my fingers and heart, and give all of my silly wishes directly to the night.

When none of those wishes came true, I realized that we learn to seek that luck as kids so we can harvest hope for the future without the hard work that is the fertilizer. We would desire the same future our ancestors craved and gave up on, or stole and stood upon.

Those starry-eyed wishes rarely came to fruition despite how hard I prayed and wished for them. Back then I probably should have been learning how to make my fears feel safer, I should have learned how to face the pain and conquer my inevitable failures.

I should have learned how to grieve my broken dreams and how to cope while still confidently chasing them. Yet instead I still stand here waiting on the clouds and what's in them to grant my selfish and childish wishes.

Why do I do that when I am right here with everything I will ever need to make them happen myself?

I guess I will learn that lesson later.

Senior Superlatives

Roses dripping fresh honey
into expectations of misfits,

life was never sweet chocolate
but the misery factory making it.

Gift wrap that gets thrown out
and lingering aches of sugary deceit,

those voted most likely to succeed
are the most likely to never leave.

Sting

Some of them think you're beautiful
until the day you think so too.
They'll do what they want to do.
They may jump out or maybe wait
until you turn around afraid.
He thinks he can if you don't say.

Some will silently hold you captive
until you stop screaming "don't."
You never feel safe anywhere alone.
You bottle your tears to survive
until your whole soul runs empty.
They see what they want to see.

The worst ones make you fall in love
until one day you uncover the lies.
You start to see through his disguise.
He will try to devour your innocent spirit
until you find courage to crush his pride.
All that's left is rage behind his eyes.

Their actions may echo clear and loud
until you shout your truth louder.
Your heart has always held your power.
Everything he does stings you hard
but you know that you are smarter.
Getting away will sting him harder.

5/22/16

Almost twenty-one and losing my balance,
tripping from the bar into the darkness.
Surrounded by couples silently fighting,
I have a new self-confidence to harness.

Our stamped hands and ripped wristbands,
a wild new desire to lose all feeling.
Being old enough has never felt better,
but I can't tell if I'm dying or healing.

Time is still among buzzing speakers,
as drinks and music create slow motion.
I watch it unfold alone in the back,
everybody is blurry and out of focus.

Stage lights flash in bloodshot eyes,
a momentary fear of going blind.

Blinking until the high starts over,
a new song plays and goes on forever.

Thoughtless sways to indistinct noise,
a room so loud I can't hear my voice.

I never enjoyed the rhapsodic facade,
but this numb feeling can now be bought.

Thorns

More giant stuffed bears and sweet cards
pile up in her bedroom with each
new season and every passing holiday.

But the vacancy inside of her grows
emptier with every flower she receives
and every petal she plucks away.

Her eyes didn't shine anymore and her
smile faded on it's own but she never
needed the petals to understand.

How does he not feel what he's done?
He's holding onto the rose so tight
that her thorns are blood on his hands.

Bridges

It was cold
      but we kissed anyway.
            It was an April afternoon under
            a foggy east coast bridge.

  I couldn't admit
      my regretful boredom.
            What the hell was that,
            that you gave in that kiss?

Every road empty
      and every light turned green.
            You made a perfect move
            but still somehow missed.

Dull

Loving without passion
is like
writing without motive,
singing without a muse,
painting without color,
speaking without thought,
existing without ambition,

It's possible,
but it's dull.

Wrong Train

We caught a train from our Manhattan hotel
because I wanted to see downtown Brooklyn.
And even after my meticulous planning
we somehow ended up on the wrong one.

It was easy to see that you were pissed off
with my questions answered in your silence.
We were lost underground somewhere in Queens
and you wouldn't look over at me once.

We got off and just went back to the room
and wasted the whole day with quiet regret.
I don't think you cared that I was hurting,
you stayed mad while I held every breath.

That was the first time I ever felt lost,
I didn't want or need your explanation.
That's when I learned to never board a train
if you are unsure of it's destination.

Paper Flowers

Your name still makes me wince
when I see it anymore.
You still haunt me in the faces
of anyone with eyes as blue
as yours.

You took most of my firsts and
most vivid teenaged sighs.
I still blame myself for going
back and forth with you so
many times.

Trying to block you from my head
and my wasted time from my mind.
But scars you left behind won't
fade and the paper flowers we made
never die.

Bathtime Baptismal

Heavy hands
create
eyelid kaleidoscopes
as my hair
floats
like silk in the wind.

I rise
from the water
with
euphoric dysfunction,

maybe this is baptism.

Maybe
this time
I'll feel clean.

Eraser

Just because
    you've been down
        the road before
doesn't mean you should go faster.

Maybe it's not
    about being a great artist
        but instead
it's about having the best eraser.

4/9/17

Lit indica in one of my hands,
your heart handed back in the other.

Neither offers any solution,
they both just make me suffer.

A torpid oblivion in the air,
as my mind craves some medicine.

Love fails to exist yet again,
but mine for you has no comparison.

I Wrote This in a Dentist's Office

Numb to the touch,

numb to the pain.

You are my weakness,

my novocaine.

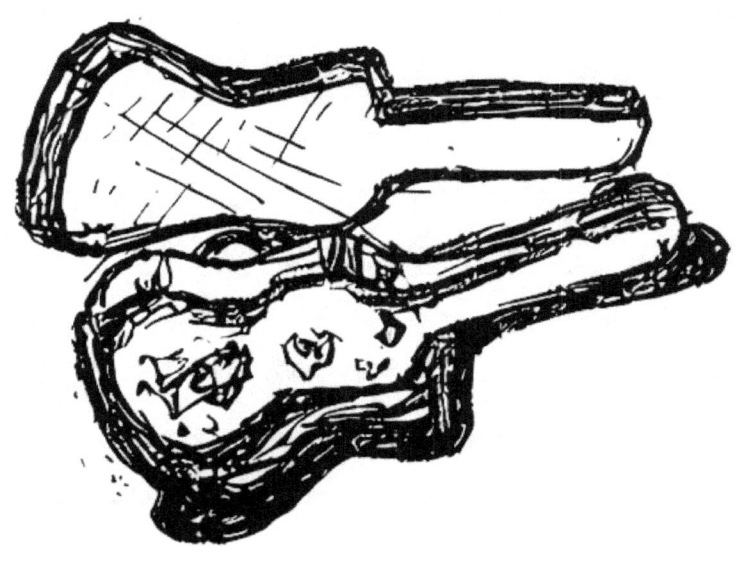

Stages

Blocks of street buskers,

playing to make some change.

Not a soul stopped to listen,

a lost world remains their stage.

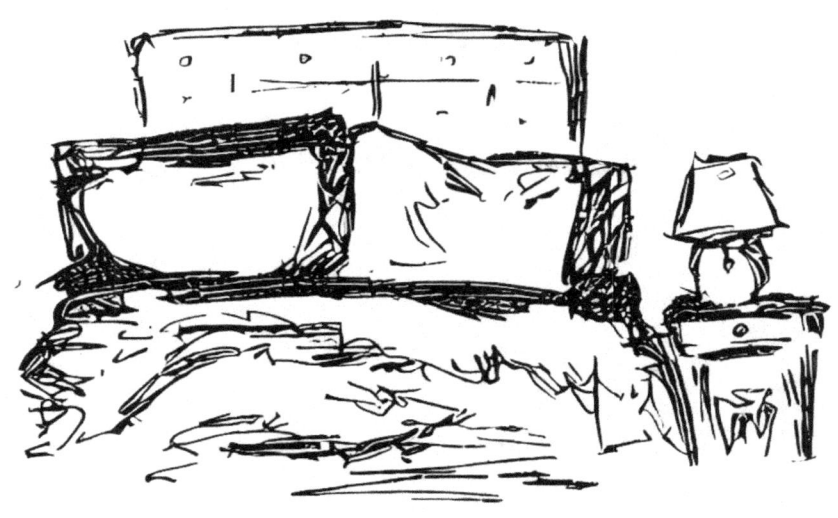

Begging

I've spent too many nights begging
you to come back to a bed of sin,
when I knew I never wanted to be
beneath your sheets to begin with.

I still wonder when I'll be asked
to come back to bed to hold,
when I might be embraced by arms
that are as welcoming as my own.

Maybe you should have tried loving
me back and begging me to stay,
before the best thing you ever had
got up, fixed her hair, and ran away.

The Moon

The moon is a fickle source of
mercurial hope that reminds me...

... Change isn't always bad.

4/20/17

A night so good
        I don't even know
        how to write about it.

                        But I did.

I regret my words
        and how they were his,
        because that night
        wasn't good at all.

                        It was the
                        beginning
                        of the end.

38

II. The Initiative

Carolina

We ran away from our comatose town
on a Sunday in the middle of June.
Reckless efforts to get there fast
but still afraid to leave too soon.

My back was turned to the rising sun
one week after I turned twenty-three.
I left the only home I had ever known
after the long goodbyes to my family.

My blue two-door Ford loaded and ready
and we came to life with the engine.
Our reverie and the stars in our eyes
kept us blinded by a brighter horizon.

A dream come true westbound journey ahead,
my mom said to be safe and enjoy the ride.
Only years later would my sister tell me
it was the only time she saw our dad cry.

Different?

"How do you know," they ask,
"you've barely shared a touch?"

        I know because nobody before
        has made me write this much.

The Darkness

Sitting in a bar full of people
drinking away happiness they lost
an eternity ago, and craving the
peace that loneliness is supposed
to bring.

The paralyzing sting of clear
spirits on our tongues, as the
bullets between our teeth help
to bite back the three words
we never say.

We watched the sun as it sank
downtown while we talked about
color theory and art, when
suddenly he looked up and said
"don't be afraid of the dark."

June

With a map in my hands,
    and valor in my veins,
        a tank full of gas,
            and these empty highways.

With firestarter hearts,
    and a new day to seize,
        my short unwashed hair
            in the car window breeze.

With the radio waves
    static on immortality,
        and 2,000 miles between
            both sedation and sanctity.

With old vacant cages,
    and rusty broken chains,
        I put all my trust in you,
            with nothing else in my way.

Tennessee

We hadn't even crossed the Carolina state line,
when you said I was speeding, so I let you drive.

Your menthol smoke floated out the cracked window,
you held every piece of me but you'd never know.

We were the kind of close that I'd never had,
you were a rollercoaster and I was your track.

It was feeling like we'd never make it there,
days of driving ahead without money or cares.

But when we finally made it through Tennessee,
that's when I noticed you watching me sleep.

Drive

How I feel with you

    is like endless conversation,

like the very first time

    without any hesitation,

like driving slow in the rain

    without a set destination.

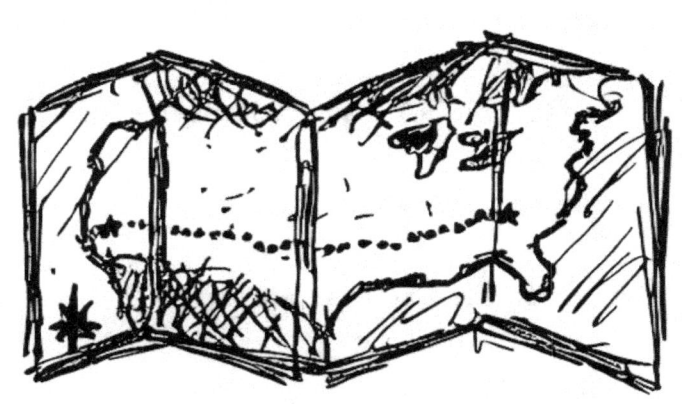

Arkansas

Wilted roses and pages unflipped,
high bar tabs for drinks unsipped.

Unfolded maps and newspaper clips,
tangled hair and untimely discontent.

Unsaid words keep us unfulfilled,
my own written are unfinished still.

Graffiti

The words inside me,
    my body can't handle.

The paper is blank,
    and I am the vandal.

Oklahoma

I never meant to hurt you,
in the end we both got hit.
It was never pain I felt,
but instead colossal guilt.

I was lost but ran anyway,
bolting as I hit the ground.
You tried to come and find me,
but I didn't want to be found.

I moved from behind to beside you,
then you saw me suddenly running.
The one thing nobody ever told me,
is everybody is running from something.

Dear Storm

Dear storm, come a little closer,
drown my melancholy in your tears,
and quiet my thoughts with thunder.

Dear storm, come a little closer,
light the dark with electric veins,
these shadows can be outnumbered.

Dear storm, please just come closer,
wash away all of my shields of fear,
and end the wars that divide lovers.

Dear storm, just a little closer,
bring some beauty among the blame,
don't let this destruction hover.

Dear storm, come a little closer,
my sullen lullabies need hysteria,
please fill my empty sky with wonder.

Room 347 (Amarillo Song)

Unfettered is the bird that flies against these cloudy
skies, wings eternally subject to break under the same
breeze that picks up the fire. Aspiring to light more than
just cigarettes with little pink lighters, with words that
expire once the drive ends and you're inspired.

A deep and meaningful silence, one that requires thought-
provoking minds and words to bind them. Roads ahead on
every road less traveled, rubbing dry our terrified eyes,
and somehow we still die trying. Rushing into a life to
strive for, like a man who climbs the mountain instead of
hiding. Untied to the harness that keeps him from flying,
he stays muted by those that restrict his shining.

Inflicting the fall of the tightrope between these highways
unwinding, and leaving all of our pain beneath and behind
them. A story told only by the chained and timed, just
wasting more time with pining and violence. Whispers at
night that lead to hope in false guidance, the weakest
embers ignited by all of your promises.

I can only vow to silence if you're mine at least for
tonight. Just take me back to room 347 at the hotel in
Amarillo and I swear I'll keep it quiet.

Roswell

Some of the best nights for me
were those nights in the desert.
    We would stare at the stars
    while listening to Def Leppard.

Twinkle lights unplugged on the patio
that we asked the bartender to turn on.
    All the distance from home we craved
    and all the freedom we could want.

We left the warm hotel in Amarillo
that had our favorite room so far.
    I'll never forget that morning in bed
    just watching you string your guitar.

You wanted to stop and visit Roswell
and I wanted to send alien postcards.
    But when we got there it was abandoned
    like a ghost town with a graveyard.

An unexplained story from the forties
where interstellar life was found.
    It wasn't some magnificent discovery,
    it was just a big hole in the ground.

Wild Horse

We wanted to see some change
so we changed the radio station.
We landed on Chris Stapleton
singing some song about salvation.

The cheap gasoline in Oklahoma City
left enough money for cheaper whiskey.
We drank away every Midwest sunset
and I prayed you'd never forget me.

Familiar radio static was humming
a broadcast from every new town.
Our wild horse dreams of the west
were finally free and on their way out.

New Mexico

He smelled like fresh pine
but tasted like liquor.
He made me want to stay
but run away even quicker.

California is burning,
let's add to the flames.
We can flick our ashes
to the beat of the pain.

No fears of inhalation,
we're already full of smoke.
We can't bend and break
if we're already broke.

You Only

Car alarms and streetlights blinking,
the asphalt illusions melting in heat,
I could never see what you were seeing.

A new road with nothing but sin ahead,
with the greatest music and company,
our terminus was the words left unsaid.

Countless miles without hot food or money,
we starved each other of touch and truth,
and I'd do it again with you, and you only.

Grand Canyon

The mirage of emptiness began to fade into his smoke clouds, and suddenly the deserted road in front of us was surrounded by never-ending mountains and valleys of red rocks. The song Sedona by Houndmouth played as our jaws unhinged at the walls of the famous terrain. We had never seen anything quite like it. Our phones kept losing signal and the music started to skip, we had no choice but to turn off our premade road trip playlists.

I wish someone had told me how expensive it is to park a car at the Grand Canyon. By the time we did and dragged our feet to the copper precipice, we were tired. Tired of driving, tired of paying to see nature, and wholeheartedly tired of the one Justin Bieber song the only station for miles played every half hour. But still, we never got tired of each other. We couldn't see into the future, but we could see all of our visions of possibility.

Tiny diners occupied by old local couples and road-tripping travelers, those overpriced french fries got us through the sting of hunger we felt for anything but food. We may have had to pay thirty bucks to park the Mustang in the rusty dirt, but it was worth every flipped penny to stand at the edge of nowhere and everywhere that day.

For a few expensive yet priceless moments, we could see beyond everything we'd ever wanted for miles.

And for a few cursory moments, we avoided falling.

Arizona

For the one who will never admit
that all of this is all about him.

If by chance he ever sees this,
he knows who he is and what he did.

He left my love in the desert wind
while all he did was just pretend.

We felt love but just as best friends,
circles of denial spun around us again.

I thought I wanted all of this,
convinced by his enticing grin.

I know that I was in love with him
but I really wish I hadn't been.

Speeding

He swerved through five lanes of LA traffic,
speeding across the highway to make the exit.

No beds or pillows but we felt like millionaires,
we giggled on the couch as he stroked my hair.

He slept on blankets next to me on the floor,
I could swear right then I never wanted more.

We decided to buy two cheap used mattresses,
across a hallway we built walls and bridges.

But one of them ended up being a waste of money,
holding onto each other was always more comfy.

We had nothing but each other that first night,
he had no idea I stayed awake and silently cried.

California

We sang in the car the whole way there,
only to find more quiet trauma to share.

From June 11th to the 11th of December,
we made our time something to remember.

We wrote the script and then we preformed it,
thinking anything was possible in California.

Interlude 1

Her

I know you hate being left all alone at night,
I held us together while still holding you tight.

The pink and sticky palms I'd get around you,
you'd never hold mine but yours were my glue.

I know you prefer love to be simple and distant,
the bottle you grip is your fear of commitment.

You can shatter all of the glass in the flames,
you're the only one who can free us from chains.

Hope (Part 1)

Staring mindlessly into the night
and waiting for shooting stars to pass.
It's the time you will never get back.

Finally giving into the loneliness
and expecting the wound to stop bleeding.
It's the rhyme without reason or meaning.

Watching the clock tick on for hours
and hoping to catch it right at 11:11.
It's the glimpse of hell on your way to heaven.

Feeling soft waves crash at your feet
and daring the tide to come in early.
It's bittersweet poison making you crave mercy.

III. The Terminus

Anesthesia

Your heart like a highway
    and eyes like champagne,
      I am lost in both,
    like getting lost on a train.

The wicked can't rest,
    no remedy for the insane.
      All that's left behind
    is anesthesia for the pain.

Stairs

No more midday wishing,

        no more pointless prayers.

No more running for nothing

        unless it gets me there.

I'm done wasting time waiting,

        I'm building my own stairs.

Wanderlust & Daydreams

I wanderlust over every inch of you,
your conniving smile and warm body.
We hide all of our sins in shadows,
but we're just friends making coffee.

You exist in daily daydream visions
that I will always shut my eyes for.
But every single time I close them,
you haunt all of my nights even more.

I can never rest easy or fall asleep,
lost in the ceiling looking for signs.
You will always be the darkest cloud
that drifts through my sleepless mind.

I'm Glad I Didn't Die Before I Met You

You create words within me
without effort or deceit.

But had you only inspired one poem,
my rhyme would still be complete.

If for some reason we never met,
it wouldn't have mattered much.

You will forever be my muse
even without a single touch.

Haunted

Too many tests I'll never pass,
so many words I can't take back.

Too many questions left unasked,
so much love that doesn't last.

Too many trains running off track,
so many hearts burned carbon black.

Too many faces behind a broken mask,
so many of us are haunted by the past.

Breathless

There are only two things
that make me feel
as breathless
as I do.

Effortless poetry
and
being alone
with you.

Why We're Alone

Every good artist is broken,
that's what makes them good.
They would rather be alone,
than be used and misunderstood.

Some hide their pain in bottles,
some too much and some a little.
Instead of spilling the truth,
they'll make you solve a riddle.

They keep it locked away in cages,
staying chained to what they've fought.
Trying to save everyone else from fear,
but their own fears are all they've got.

Love Drunk

                    I fell for blue eyes when I
             was young, that was the night I fell madly
               in love. 2 AM at Denny's when I was told I was
          never enough, that was the night I stopped believing
               in love. It happened again and all of my scars
                    stung, that was when I completely gave up on
             finding love. I've heard the third time's a charm in
    passion and lust, and once again I nearly fell for white
          lies of love. I know he only wanted me when he was
                    drunk, only now do I see none of them were ever
               in love.

Bubbles

Hidden sadness is too much trouble.

You don't want to talk about it,
but you still want them to care.

Stuck inside so many damn bubbles.

You never wanted to have to admit,
you have to pop them to get there.

There is a true
friendship betwee

Another Song

Comparing our favorite paintings
in your bedroom floor until morning.
We kept losing track of the time
and kept ignoring every warning.

You tried your hardest to teach me
how to play your acoustic guitar.
My dumb tiny hands began to cramp
so we stopped and talked about stars.

You showed me your favorite albums
from Tool's 10,000 Days to Sublime.
You would hold me and without fail,
I fell asleep every single time.

A late night takeout fortune cookie
made us laugh because it wasn't wrong.
We had a true and sincere friendship
and now it has composed another song.

Dreams & Nightmares

Expectations make us believe
that everything is better in our dreams.

We refuse to open our eyes and see
until we wake up to our own loud screams.

Reality fights irrational belief
but even our nightmares can set us free.

Playgrounds

Scratched up knees
and princess dresses,
chasing princes and
failing to impress them.

An old childhood cycle
continues to spin,
life is just a playground
where nobody wins.

Games

I've heard that you have to lose
                    before you can appreciate winning.

But does anyone still enjoy the game
                    or is there something we're missing?

The finish line is just within reach
                    but none of our wheels are spinning.

There is beauty hidden in losing,
                    the only way to truly fail is quitting.

Love & Libation

Drink like artists.

Love like poets.

Quantum Entanglement

We're hovering over the thin line between
myth and creation.

Floating above this spasmodic lust but below
ethereal perception.

Our distance is hunger with satisfaction and
sensuality with thirst.

A separation of souls the universe denied
quickly became my curse.

IV. The Craving

July

Stuck and still lost somewhere not right,
sun shining but providing nowhere to hide.

It seems I only like California at night.

Hands

Eyes shut, mouths are hushed,
a quiet night, my cheeks flush.

Urges unravel, minds are closed,
lost in you, I bloom into a rose.

Warm skin, a sweet static touch,
lips move, but we don't say much.

Breath tingling, it's therapeutic,
biting down as your hands make music.

Demons

You can't destroy your demons alone,
they only desire your quiet demise.

I want to show you lights in the dark,
but you still refuse to open your eyes.

Blue

I once met a boy with bright blue hair,
he looked like a modern-day Peter Pan.

I only knew him for about two weeks,
but he reminded me of new beginnings.

I still think about him when it rains,
even though I don't remember his name.

I wonder if he's still happily unique,
or if his band still plays bars in Long Beach.

I wonder if he ever remembers me,
and if his hair is still the color of dreams.

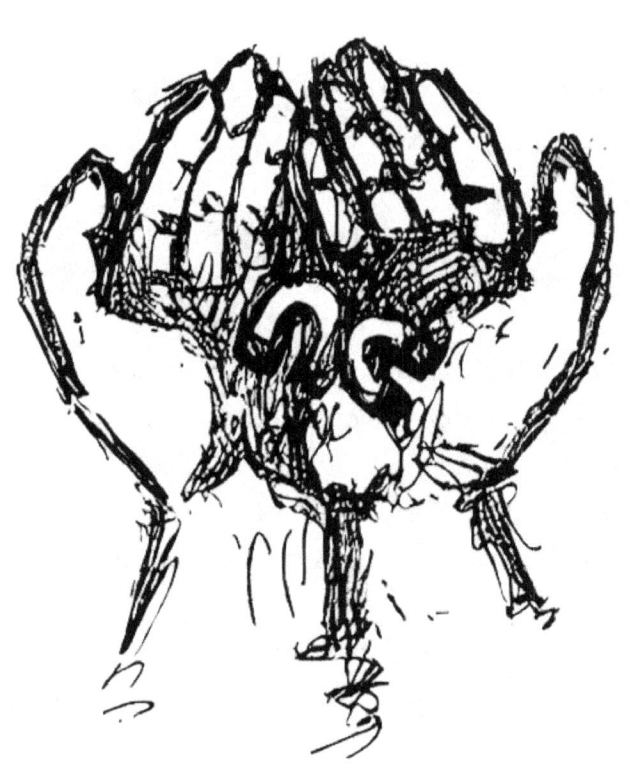

Magnets

We're like two backwards magnets
just forcing ourselves together.
One of us will eventually be ready
but the other one could never.

So desperate to be that close
saying we want to work in unison.
But the tiniest bit of resistance
pulls us further apart again.

We're almost just within grasp
of the connection magnets demand.
It's right there, just out of reach,
but I'm the only one holding out my hands.

Fears & Constellations

I'm stuck here with a runaway heart
and burn holes in my shirtsleeves,
my every breath is a plea for air
and every minute is time's thief.

Taking a million steps through
my old fears and constellations,
they remind me of big kid slides
where scary risk was revelation.

Maybe I was entirely wrong and
maybe he was never Mr. Right, but
at least he taught me how to run
and how to put up a good fight.

Hopeful Poets

Numbing your cold shoulder
as I read my poetry aloud.
You hardly took a breath,
you barely made a sound.

We spent way too long
pushing through the days.
Wasting all of our time
waiting on clocks to change.

Still hoping that someday
I might just be enough.
Praying the pain will prove
our lust was never love.

Mystery

A dark pub and all of it's walls tiled
with bottled fortitude and apathy galore.
Spinning our stools and clinking glasses,
we dismiss memories to make room for more.

Everyone's lips are eager and parted
for excessive liquid anesthetics.
We all came here to forget how to feel
and that's all we'll remember of it.

The noises are distant and clogged
and the smoky chatter makes it foggy.
All of our senses will soon diminish
but it'll still taste bitter and salty.

Mouths will trickle their risky secrets
of torrential love and hidden infidelity.
Callous hearts will always leak the truth
when they mix their mystery with whiskey.

Sheet Music

My lips and tongue still
taste just as sweet as you.
Both left dry and empty like
the bottle we powered through.

Your slow and rough hands
tangled up in my hair.
We penned our song that night
while completely unaware.

Melodies etched into memory
and left staining these sheets.
Eventually it may wash away but
those words will always bleed.

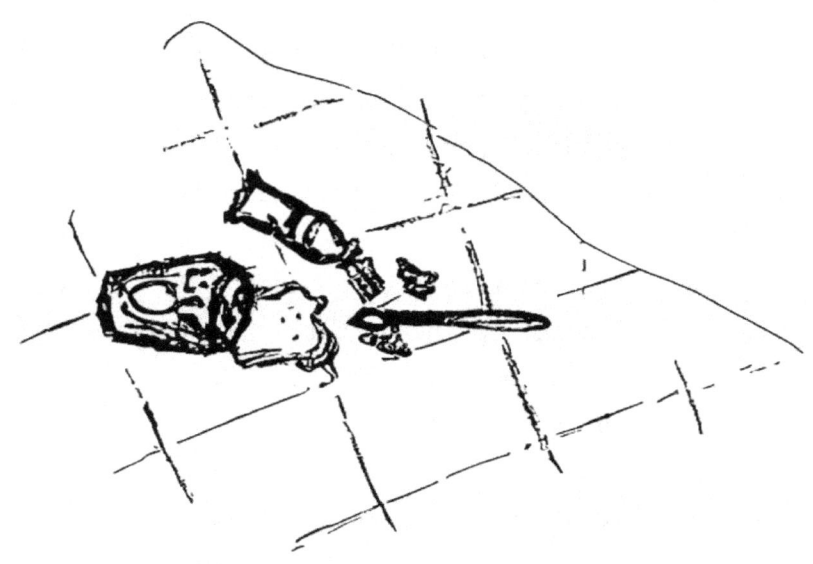

August

Happiness was that drive
back from the bar too late,
  or the day you sang to me
  through the sliding glass door.
    It was a joke but it wasn't.

Happiness was dancing to Chance
the Rapper in the hallway,
  or the night we spilled paint
  and beer on the kitchen floor.
    It was never consistent.

Happiness was listening to
old rock instrumentals play,
  or harmonizing with the sirens
  outside because we were bored.
    It was love in an apartment.

Happiness was cheap whiskey
and heartbeat lullabies all day,
  or all of the songs you learned
  because they were songs I adored.
    Songs we once knew by heart,
    now I skip them the quickest.

The Broad

He was the priceless masterpiece
at that Los Angeles art museum.
We were surrounded by frames,
but all I could see was him.

I could have stared for hours
while he studied canvas and brush.
But at The Broad, just like the art,
I could look but I couldn't touch.

Let's Get Lost

Let's get lost in Laurel Canyon,
winding roads and spinning wheels without direction.

Let's get lost in our own paradise,
laughing like kids until the middle of the night.

Let's get lost in downtown lights,
so full yet so damn empty and we don't know why.

Let's get lost in Sweet Baby James,
playing it loud as the tin roof meets the rain.

Let's get lost in each other,
ignoring our feelings with the moon as our cover.

Let's get lost in this quiet moment,
just tangled up in right now and how we spend it.

The Rain

After putting yourself through hell,
you stop feeling the acidity of pain.

After standing in the sun for so long,
you start to miss the comfort of rain.

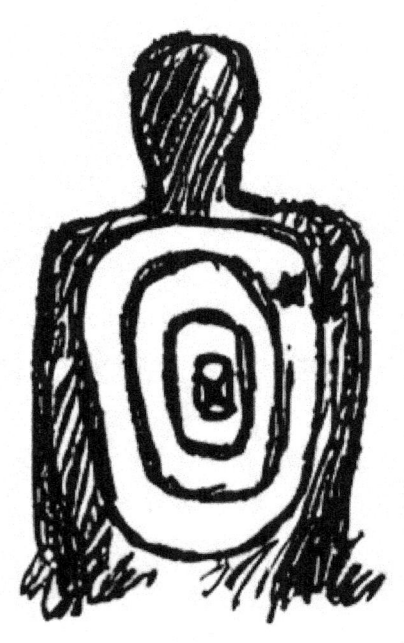

Safety

Fervor secured like bullets
in the chamber of your gun.
You focus and stare down the barrel.

You miss every single shot
with your near perfect aim.
You intentionally avoid the shrapnel.

You claim to stop and wait
for a convenient moment.
She's the target but you won't hit her.

And just when it seems
you turned off the safety,
You still won't pull the damn trigger.

The Girl

I keep hearing that old City and
Colour song you'd always sing.
How stupid of me to ever think
you could be singing it for me.

You always talked about the girl,
the one who haunted your past.
The girl you named your guitar
after, just to make her last.

I was the one you held at night
under thin blankets on the floor.
Back then I could still pretend
I was the girl you played it for.

I never asked for diamond rings,
strings of pearls, or even love.
But you kept me strung up anyway
while I just wanted to be enough.

You never wrote a song for me,
not a single verse or bridge.
My wish to be the girl you loved
was just another wasted wish.

Interlude 2

His

I hate feeling this broken so much.
Why am I like this? Every shot another crutch.

Ignoring the boxes I pack myself into,
I think I belong here and deserve the abuse.

I wish this bullshit was easier to forget,
I hate that my promises are just your regrets.

I bottle it up and burn myself to the core.
I want to be loved but I can't feel anymore.

Hope (Part 2)

I hope one day something
comes out of these words and
this sadness I perpetuate.

        I hope one day something
        left reminds me why I should
        have loved you and stayed.

V. The Haze

High

Rope burns char your name into my heart,
from where you suspended it, then cut it
down and ran away.
Trying to channel this hurt you created,
but you swear you didn't mean it, so I just
stay in bed all day.

Veins like tunnels full of the rubble you
left behind, while you took the easy way out
as you watched me fade.
What do I tell my mom when she asks how
you are, and I say I don't know, because you
didn't want to stay?

Where is the best place to hide all of these
feelings, high up in my closet in a box with
your worn old clothes?
Why does falling ferociously in love feel
elevated, like the best kind of high, when I
feel so goddamn low?

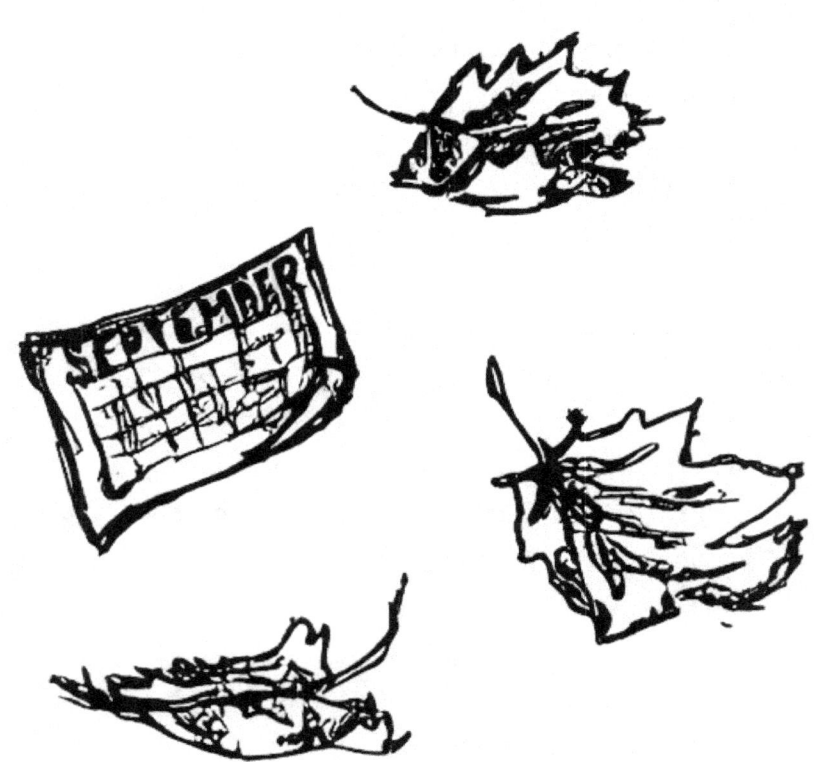

158

September

Effortlessly,

you were

September.

Effortlessly,

I fell

with the

leaves.

Pleading

Please.

Please stop giving me beautiful things
to write about at three in the morning.
When we're drunk and I'm wrapped in you,
before all the alarms and storm warnings.

Please.

Please stop holding me tight for hours
while we only exist in fleeting moments.
I'm telling myself this time you'll remember,
living only in your memory is my punishment.

Please.

162

Never Have I Ever

I have never felt anything quite like lighting
up with you, and my world catching fire while
it also burned to the ground.

I never wanted to let myself love someone the
way that I loved you, but now I can see that
you just wanted me around.

I have never wanted anything more than for you
to show up at my door, where you'd grab my hand
and pull me into the hallway.

I never expected this endless pain, like seeing
your face and feeling alive again, as my heart
continues to break anyway.

Static

I know how these sad films end
so I stopped watching the movies.

You paid everything but attention
and I was always just a groupie.

Obsolete black and white scenes
became an old glitching static.

We fade out like shitty scripts
where happy endings never happen.

Halfway

Our first kiss was an accident,
dancing to traffic on the balcony.
You teased a kiss with your lips,
and I stole it from you anyway.

Since then everything is broken,
the most perplexing shade of gray.
We never talked about it back then,
so I guess it will stay that way.

Trying to tolerate my own avoidance,
I ignore it as the next song plays.
I know I will never understand it,
and it's easier for you to run away.

Give me back our flawless friendship,
before I fucked it all up in one day.
Tell me you're waiting in the kitchen,
please tell me you'll meet me halfway.

Gingerbread Houses

Gingerbread houses
brewing sweet lies.
    It looks like heaven
    but in candied disguise.

        Just two kids lost
        in careless disregard.
            Unaware they're trapped
            right where they are.

            Enchantment is never
            as lovely as it seems.
                Turning all the locks
                but losing the keys.

            Breadcrumb trails
            in a forest of dreams.
        Every legend says to
        stay out of the trees.

        Gingerbread houses
        dripping in illusion.
Behind endearing doors
lies nothing but ruin.

Chloroform

I fell asleep thinking of you again.
I accidentally turned desire to dream,
the same one again, a painful scene.

I never notice it's just my delusion.
For a second it seems so damn real,
I can see and hear you, even feel.

A brief and gentle hallucination.
I knew I'd forget it just as it ended,
waking up knowing I can't extend it.

This euphoria is just like chloroform.
Easy to make if you don't rest enough,
but suffocating even after one puff.

Habits

Subconscious kicks,
my nails bitten.
Anxious ticks
and pages written.

Clenched teeth,
my tapping feet.
Avoiding eyes
dancing in streets.

Darker nights
after days of blue.
All lines blur
when I'm with you.

Addicted to it,
this zapping static.
You have become
my worst habit.

Pollution

When simply breathing becomes a chore,
lungs like balloons and ribs like pins.

You light one up in search of solitude,
but you can't clear the smoke within.

The polluted air is all in your head,
still unsure if the flames are a joke.

You scream into the sky for some rain,
but it never read the words you wrote.

October

I stuffed the half-smoked
cigarette I stole from you
back deep into my pocket.

I tip-toed outside alone
into a neon night with an
adolescent innocence.

Just like your Pall Malls,
the tight grip you had on
me also made me choke.

But now I'm here shaking,
craving your whole pack,
and I don't even smoke.

Shattered

This life led us to make art and create,
we only wanted 27 but we still got 28.

White lighters crushing pills and dreams,
taking a risk while we rip at the seams.

Silent penthouse bathrooms devoid of life,
clandestine cries and no will to survive.

Our wins dwindle like they never mattered,
life is a shitshow we would rather shatter.

Old Stories

You and I fell in love by dumb chance,
like old stories where nothing dies.

You didn't want anyone to find out,
so accusations of love stayed denied.

The light at the end blinded us both,
like old stories of Hollywood suicide.

Smoke & Flames

Flames have a way of creating
persistent destruction
in the most bittersweet content.

Keeping the fire under control
seems beyond hopeless
as the smoke disappears in the wind.

Bodies

I am just another body

       chasing shadows in the moon.

We're the streetlamps at night

       that flicker and die too soon.

Stranded

Late night laughter tangled under sheets,
those rare weekends purified long weeks.

Neon warning signs danced pink and blue,
but I couldn't focus on anything but you.

Lust turned to love and turned upside down,
it left me defenseless and stumbling around.

Things will come and go, people run away,
maybe I could have convinced you to stay.

They all said this affair would never last,
now I'm alone in your shirt and in the past.

Tipsy sips before trips on unplanned flights,
I finally found peace from up high at night.

I am no longer stranded in empty airport bars,
it's far easier to fall in love with the stars.

Remember?

Remember that night
you begged me to stay?
You passed out but in
your arms I laid awake.

I could never say no and
I could never fall asleep.
You wanted all of my love
but you never wanted me.

Radio Stations

Take me back
    to no worries
        and empty roads.

To repetitive
    old folk songs
        on desert radios.

VI. The Exit

When

Unseen hands around my neck,
buckled up but willing to wreck.

Stars offer asylum to our sins,
we pour drinks but never say when.

Homesick Ghosts

The higher the fall,
the harder the blow.
Church after the bar
wearing the same clothes.

Looking for ourselves
and a little bit of hope.
Praying for guidance
or some kind of growth.

We collected the seeds
but forgot how to sow.
Faking smiles all day
and no one even knows.

Too empty to move on
so we go with the flow.
We float through life
like homesick ghosts.

Enough

I miss the incandescent way
you used to look over at me,
and your natural reassurance
when I felt helplessly weak.

When you would drink enough
to have nothing to regret,
when I didn't care at all
what anyone thought or said.

When I was gullible enough
to fall for your sweet lies,
and you were too stubborn
to spare love or compromise.

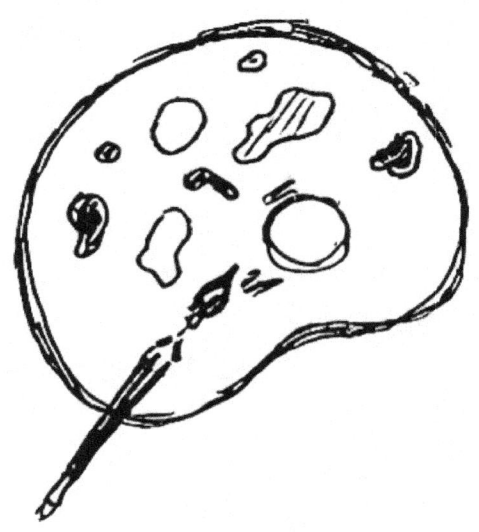

Saturation

You were carefully charming
and so beautifully cunning,
as you stopped all of my
saturation from running.

Like the middle of our late
night watercolor paintings,
all of my color pooled up
but I dried out waiting.

November

Luminous illusions and never-ending reruns,
it seems Hollywood's more fucked up than us.

We never stopped looking and didn't give up,
but this city feels too damn hard to trust.

We chased every dream and didn't find one,
almost through hell, just one more month.

Oh

Forgotten feelings

without forgiveness,

forbidden futures

and fears of failure.

Our hands intertwined

but tied behind us,

the ropes feel weak

but remain unsevered.

For Show

You put on a pretty persona,
you put on a really good show.

Even when you left me cold and alone,
I was still always in the front row.

Pessimist

Love is almost always
some unrequited bullshit.
All shiny and wrapped up,
optimistic and moonlit.

We can love more or less,
we are all just people.
We can give all or nothing,
but it is never equal.

Ship

I am a shipwreck.
My head a stormy wave beneath clouds,
every creak in the deck feels so loud.

I am a shipwreck.
A tired crash to shore without warning,
a quiet plea despite the sea roaring.

I am a shipwreck.
Memories lost to sips and clumsy falls,
the empty bottle had a message after all.

Apartment Rendezvous

The very last time
your lips met mine
you were trying to keep my tears from falling.

I was your favorite,
you said you meant it,
you held me tight and called me your darling.

The love for you I kept,
you never would accept,
all you wanted was an apartment rendezvous.

But you wanted to go,
and said you didn't know,
no wonder I never felt good enough for you.

Reality

Out of sleepless nights
   and tossed out roaches,
      a reckless reality grew.

   My ecstasy like smoke
  left cold and fleeting,
the night I needed you.

I Thought

This is what I wished for,
it's all I've ever wanted.

Love and endless daydreams,
I thought I finally got it.

It's everything I ever craved,
but I feel so damaged and small.

All of those things I wanted,
I don't think I wanted at all.

Me & You

I held onto your words
  when you would never hold me.

I let you twist my arms
  while yours never reached for me.

I wanted all of your love
  but it was never meant for me.

Watercolor & Whiskey

Mixing my cheap watercolor and whiskey,
a good medium to ignore feeling guilty.

It turns out paint is flammable too,
both are hazards as dangerous as you.

I never wanted this masterpiece to burn,
destruction is something I never unlearned.

You stole my passion and didn't earn it,
you are the drug that I can never quit.

December

He was the highest definition channel
in my electric antenna static heart.

But in the end it doesn't matter much
when it storms and the power goes dark.

Captive

I melted in the fire
of our very first hello,

but you let me drown
beneath waves of goodbye.

You avoid the duplicity
dripping from your skin,

still holding me captive
even though I'm untied.

Page 72

The midnight stars above our
apartment watched as I flipped
through pages that felt like
they were written for me.

Weightless cigarette ashes fell
into the spine as smoke floated
from my lips with a new secrecy
that I swore myself to keep.

I had to stop reading and
bookmark page 72 because
it reminded me too much of
being wanted and held by you.

The only taste you ever left
in my mouth was the bitterness
of burning filters and so much
more life to love and lose.

North Star

While I was lost and looking
for the North Star that night,

I found the brightest star instead
shooting past the crescent moon.

But it could have been a meteor
or a plane just passing through,

because it came and went
just as quickly as you.

Interlude 3

The Lovers

The lovers wanted their stars to align,
but forgot that stars could still blind.

They felt the fire and it's warm touch,
so lost in love that they only felt lust.

Turning each other into explosive sparks,
they hit the target but missed the mark.

Unlearning toxic cycles seems impossible,
but courage to change will remain optional.

Hope (Part 3)

I hope she knows how fucking lucky she is
to feel your heartbeat and your soft kiss.

I hope she knows to hold you while you sleep
and how much extra reassurance you will need.

I hope she can give you everything you want
and knows how much you love Stevie Ray Vaughan.

I hope she can show you those perfect things
that I know you could never find within me.

        I hope she is easier for you to love,
and that no matter how much she gives,
               nothing will ever be enough.

        I hope she sees what you'll never get over,
and that you don't always mean it,
               when you tell her you love her.

VII. The Loss

Hey, I'm Back

First one lit from

    a brand new pack.

Everybody misses you

    until you come back.

Tuner

It's worse than I could have imagined,
it's as if nothing ever even happened.

I can't seem to forget our vast history
or erase you from my favorite memories.

I told you back then I knew I'd lose you,
not wanting to believe you knew it too.

I wanted to tune up your dissonant heart
like how I'd watched you tune your guitar.

It always sounded off no matter what I did.
Every time I had it, you would rearrange it.

Even bad strings can still write good songs,
melodies that feel right but sound so wrong.

Sparks

I feel my breath slip away
in the burning orange light.

I tear and rip at the walls
but the paper is glued on tight.

All of the deadbolts are locked,
windows boarded up and sealed.

I can't escape these flames,
so hot they're melting steel.

This fire never needed sparks,
all it took were the lies you spoke.

You tossed lit matches right inside
knowing I would go up in smoke.

Home To You

It didn't last very long,
no dreams of ours came true.

But even on my worse days
and my nights of navy blue,

to me it still meant everything,
just coming back home to you.

Heartburn & Heartbreak

Have you ever been so lost and broken
that tears don't even stream down?
Your voice feels stuck in a silent film
and your body in a California drought.

Like suffocating in a tiny room of mirrors,
my mouth and lungs filled with more regret.
I was clouded by my naive wishful thinking
but now I just wish that we had never met.

The burn was rapid and unbearable
like the taste of Fireball on my lips.
All I got was heartburn and heartbreak
when it left me feeling as wasted as you did.

Phantom

I hope I'm the phantom touch
you feel in nightmares
that your dreams try hard to fight.

I hope I'm the ghostly arm
you feel holding you
while we both sleep alone tonight.

Uninvited

You're the roadblock
in my way,
the ricochet through
my brain.

                              You're the chipped paint
                                      in my finish,
                              the fire I can never
                                  fully extinguish.

You're just a hiccup
in my chest,
you are my heart's
uninvited guest.

Knocking

I always end up back on your porch,
holding a cigarette, knocking on your door.
Waking up your mom as the rain pours.

Begging to hold you just once more,
like all those nights we slept on the floor.
I just need to know that this isn't war.

Replacements

I can't fill all the silence with sound
and I envy those who can.
Instead I fill the void with bad habits
while you got up and ran.

These replacements never seem to work,
unfortunately I am aware.
Being alone never bothered me much until
I was lonely with you there.

I was doing perfectly fine before you,
I was winning a race uphill.
But nobody can pick me up from the fall
except the one who never will.

Matches

All of my thoughts
    are just more
        fucked up truths,

    and all of my
        Tinder matches
            look like you.

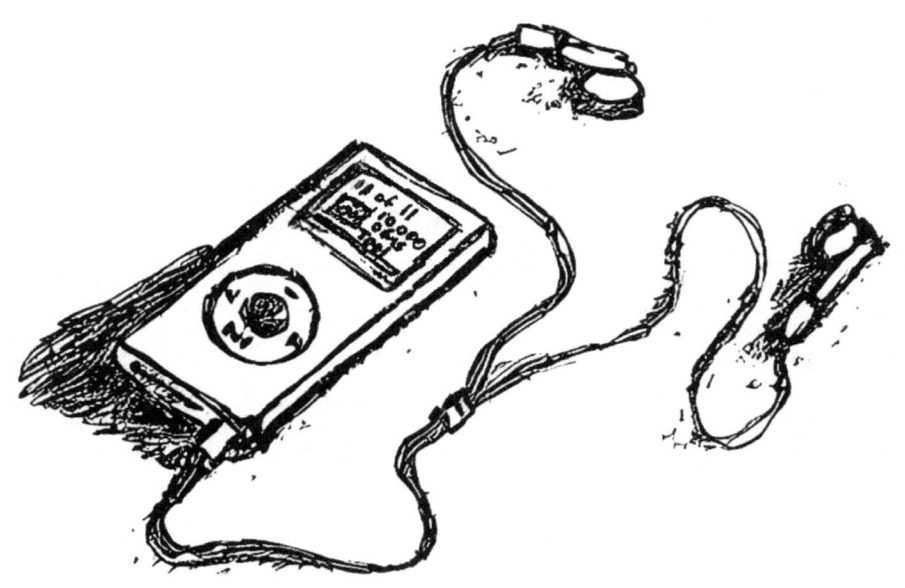

Bands

I miss mornings spent
listening to bands I
don't like with you,

because now those old
stupid bands are all
that I can listen to.

Thoughts

Between the empty bottle
and an overflowing ashtray,
I'm in the corner of the shower
and trying not to go insane.

Sat cradling my shaky knees
as the water mixes with tears,
all to the beat of this song
that's helping them run clear.

The Band Camino's lyrics
bringing back what we were,
a song still stuck in my head
that makes me wish I was her.

I still need you,

I still need you,

I
still
need
you.

Mom

There's a fine line between love
and dependency, but who will let
me love them if nobody needs me?

Misery-filled days and nicotine
smoke nights, who will still be
there if I don't win the fight?

Reminiscing on when popsicles mended
broken hearts and scraped knees, when
going home to mom could still fix me.

Both

Memories and mistakes;

I miss making

both of them

by your side.

The Endings

I took down pictures,
ripped up letters,
tried convincing myself
I could do better.

I washed my sheets,
rearranged my room,
tried scrubbing away
every ounce of you.

I could see signs
but also blissful sin,
all of your sharp turns
turned out to be dead ends.

Hums

I learned your touch as easily as lyrics
and it was familiar within a single day.
We would sing while you strummed softly
the Shakey Graves song you always played.

I felt nostalgia manifest in your hands,
with you and the tune stuck in my head.
Now the remaining echo sounds so obscure
but I can still hear every word you said.

All I remember is our distant yesterdays
when we never stumbled or skipped a beat.
I haven't heard that duet in a long time
but it still plays in my mind on repeat.

I'm not sure I'll ever sing aloud again
and I turn the radio off when I'm alone.
There's too many sweet hums I can't forget
while I wait for this to feel like home.

Titanic

I am the iceberg,
        you are the ship.

Your heavy touch
        caressed my lips.

You disappeared
        into deep blues.

I'm trying to swim
        but where are you?

Edits

Oversaturated daydreams with you
turned into blurry nightmares alone.
I wish I could edit you out of my head
as easily as the pictures in my phone.

An invisible silhouette will still linger
even after I crop you completely out.
But how can I delete memories of a love
that you never wanted to talk about?

VIII. The Legacy

Destructible

Killing people with your kindness
only works if they're destructible.

I don't have anything to confess
but I'm stuck wedged in the middle.

Feeling both put together and a mess,
pleasing everyone is impossible.

Trails

Peace is the sunlight through thick
trees that beams into me and shines.

We wasted our time trying to escape the
forest when the forest was always mine.

Looking everywhere for a path to follow
home and finding everything except you,
                              the trails,
                              and time.

Bar Singer

You were playing guitar at my local dive bar,
I was getting tipsy, trying not to overthink.
You covered every song that lowered my guard,
while I covered the tab of my own cheap drinks.

You played some of my favorite old classics,
I took sip after shot as you started to blur.
You hummed tunes I thought I only imagined,
I felt like the victim of a melodic saboteur.

You sang for dozens of red-eyed regulars,
I was still trying not to think about him.
You saw me ask the bartender for another,
I was sinking so all I could do was swim.

You began strumming the start of Rhiannon,
I stumbled out to walk home in a neon glow.
Your music chased me as I left you abandoned,
but I can't stay if he still headlines my show.

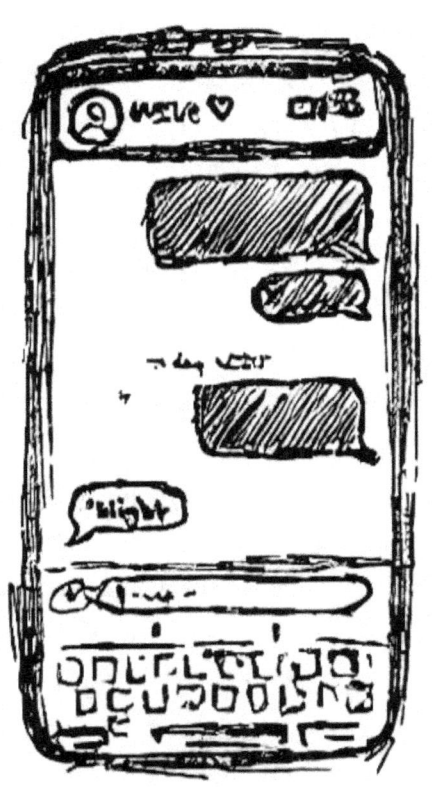

'Night

The stars won't fall
        just because you want them to.

You should never wonder
        if someone cares about you.

Make all the wishes you want,
        trust me, I've already tried.

They'll tell you how much they care
        in how they tell you goodnight.

Smoke & Intimacy

They'll never tell you
how meaningless
intimacy is
when
you are
in love
but only
with
them.

They are
the fire
and
anyone else
disappears
in
the smoke
you
keep
within.

Pending

Is it really so strange to love
every couple that resembles us?

But they seem a little different
because they can love with trust.

Why can't all stories have happy endings?

A home for sale but it's always pending.

Sunday

I walk with my head down
to avoid being in the way.

I feel like the propaganda
for a sad and rainy Sunday.

Surrounded by so much noise,
I flinch at every alarm beep.

My ears start ringing along
to muffled music and tire squeaks.

The foggy droplets on headlights
light my way to somewhere new.

I know the way out of this storm
but all I'm missing is you.

Dreams

I can't roll to the other side of the bed
because it feels like you should be there.

With an extra pillow, words we never said,
and half of the heart you wanted to spare.

Wide awake and praying my love you'll keep
but nobody ever stays to calm my screams.

Every night the clock says I need some sleep
but at least I can never remember my dreams.

White Ink Pen

I was just a white ink pen
useless and drying on paper.

You were just blank pages
waiting on their painter.

Those west coast sunsets
were full of our despair.

California never felt like home,
but it did when you were there.

Timeless

Isn't it so sad
    to think about
        how many things
            could have been
            perfect,
      if only
    the timing
had been.

New Moons

My soul evaporates more with every
second spent away from you. Every
psychedelic daydream keeps me
wishing for a starry night. A
chained up moon beckons me from
this deep sleeplessness and into the
darkness where I finally feel safe.

Technicolor Serenade

I lived in your technicolor serenade.

All I ever wanted was to be your girl
but all you cared about was getting laid.

You scored the beat and wrote the words.

You were the voice you never gave me
that you made sure nobody ever heard.

Your shield of dismissal became my war.

You never earned or deserved my bloodshed,
I won and I don't cry for you anymore.

Humid

He was her most fatal dose
of both sin and serenity,
the coldest heart offering
a breeze in the humidity.

He was a willing accomplice
who had anything but empathy,
once she stopped forcing it
she found her serendipity.

That Night

Long nights and conversations we never got through.
It started that night and that night, you knew.

We talked in my car until windows fogged the view.
It happened that night and that night, I knew.

I tried to make you quit but now I smoke them too.
You lost me that night and that night, we both knew.

You left the party with her to go and get screwed.
It ended that night and that night, everyone knew.

Now you are just words and pages I finally outgrew.
Your darkness lit me up so tonight, I'm thanking you.

Let Me

Let me find beauty in the misfortune I face,
I want to believe that not everything is fake.

Let me hear the truth in all lies and laughs,
and see positive light in negative photographs.

Let me abandon what isn't worthy and toss it,
to be humble in success and thoughtful in losses.

Let me forget those who left me in a dark place,
and instead hold tight to the ones who stayed.

Let me make good decisions and some bad ones too,
and to accept all the lessons I learn when I do.

Let me keep looking up even when I'm at the top,
I will always be climbing, just don't let me stop.

Today

I want to go to the mountains,
take me to a safe seclusion.
I want to find a real escape,
where I can live in delusion.

I want to fly up to the stars,
and believe in all their fire.
I want to see it all from there,
what could possibly feel higher?

Pick me up, take me out of here,
I'll pay whatever I have to pay.
Take me to a place where I can float,
I want to go, and I want to go today.

Alive

Anything he destroyed is just backup noise,

watered down with paint water and a brush.

A canvas that's new again but this time alive,

and now it's all mine and there's no rush.

Perfection

You can still seek out perfection

without crumbling in it's absence.

                    Sometimes in order to share your art

                    you have to heal from what created it.

Salvation

Staring at the moving moon and tire tracks,
I wished for this but I'll never go back.

My memory falls to breaking my car's window,
or to the night we wrote a song in Amarillo.

I still taste your cheap whiskey on my lips,
I never thought it would be something I'd miss.

What I was looking for was never there to find,
we never found salvation in that city limit sign.

The End
(of one story)

Index

Acknowledgements

Mom and Dad for their support through not just the process of publishing my first book, but also every heartbreak I ever went through. Their love and advice have gotten me further than I could have ever managed on my own. I love them for raising me to always be true to myself and for teaching me to only accept mutual and meritorious love.

Nana and Papaw and my two sisters for always being lovingly critical in everything I do and always telling me when a boy is bad news. For helping to heal the wounded girl that came back from each painful low. My soul would be empty without them and I love them more than they will ever know.

My best friend Taylor for helping me proofread all 150+ of my original hand-typed poems and never hesitating to tell me if I messed up the grammar or if something sounded weird. Grateful for a friend who is always the ear that listens when my ADHD mind has ridiculous themes and ideas to toss around.

My baby blue 1970's Brother Charger 11 typewriter that I named Tulip, which was the extremely advanced technology I used to type my first complete manuscript. And my dog Zoey, for tolerating the repetitive and obnoxious sounds of typewriter keys slapping paper for hours on end and weeks at a time, and hanging out with me anyway.

The boys who got me to where I am today and especially the one who got into my heart and under my skin enough to inspire this particular story. Even if it didn't end as I would have hoped back then, it still taught me countless lessons about life and love and how to channel every deep emotion into my art and words. They taught me how to know what I deserve.

Without the unpleasant pain, there is no bittersweet gain. Thank you to anyone who got me through both.

www.ingramcontent.com/pod-product-compliance
Lightning Source LLC
Chambersburg PA
CBHW071138130626
46553CB00004B/1427